MW01122276

Sibs

Sibs

by
Diane Flacks
&
Richard Greenblatt

Playwrights Canada Press
Toronto•Canada

Playwrights Canada Press
54 Wolseley Street, 2nd Floor
Toronto, Ontario CANADA M5T 1A5
416-703-0013   fax 416-703-0059   info@puc.ca   http://www.puc.ca

Playwrights Canada Press acknowledges the support of The Canada Council for the Arts for our publishing programme and the Ontario Arts Council.

Cover photo of Diane Flacks and Richard Greenblatt by Greg Tjepkema.
Production Editor: Jodi Armstrong

National Library of Canada Cataloguing in Publication Data

Flacks, Diane
  Sibs

ISBN 0-88754-623-4

I. Greenblatt, Richard, 1952- II. Title.

PS8561.L264S52 2002   C812'.6   C2001-904237-X
PR9199.4.F54S52 2002

First edition: February 2002.
Printed and bound by AGMV Marquis at Quebec, Canada.

The authors would like to dedicate this play to their siblings:
Daniel Flacks
Laura Flacks-Narrol
Lewis Furey

The authors would like to acknowledge Urjo Kareda, Andy McKim, Kate Lushington, Leah Cherniak, Rick Sacks, Savoy Howe, and especially Alisa Palmer in the development of this script.

Sibs was first produced in Toronto at the Tarragon Theatre from March 7 to April 16, 2000 with the following cast:

SHE	Diane Flacks
HE	Richard Greenblatt
MUSICIAN	Rick Sacks

Director	Alisa Palmer
Set and Costume design	Glenn Davidson
Lighting Design	Andrea Lundy
Original music	Rick Sacks
Movement coach	Savoy Howe
Fight director	James Binkley
Stage manager	Arwen MacDonnell

Movement choreography was originally by Pam Johnson.

SIBS

Music.

SHE and HE enter the stage, and walk into the living room. They are in their forties.

HE sits and SHE stands, exhausted. Pause. SHE sits.

HE   Oh God. I am so exhausted. So, are you really gonna call her?

SHE   I'd love to keep in touch with her. Wouldn't you?

HE   It's kinda weird. Like, what is she, like who – it's not like she's our stepmother or anything. She's Cherise, Dad's girlfriend.

SHE   She's a nice lady. She was very good to Dad.

HE   She was actually, I'll give her that. Like Dad really... I think he loved her. (*little laugh*) She's not like Mom was though, huh? Not like Mom at all.

SHE takes the coverings off the mirror upstage.

SHE   God, I look old.

HE   You look fine.

SHE crosses downstage and looks out.

Leave all of that. There's a cleaning woman coming tomorrow. Don't bother.

SHE   Well, we shouldn't leave the food out.

HE   Why?

SHE   It's food.

HE   What are you gonna do, take it back to the hotel with you?

SHE   Can you help me put the cushions back on the couch?

SHE exits. HE stays sitting.

HE   Please would you leave it? We don't have to do anything. No one's coming here or living here or anything. We don't have to do it. Leave it!

HE starts to join her. SHE's done. SHE returns.

SHE   OK. That's it. That's done.

HE   OK. That's it. Let's sit down.

They re-enter the living room area and sit down. Long pause.

HE   We're orphans now.

SHE   (*almost simultaneous*) I gotta get out of here. Let's get outta here. Can you call me a cab?

HE   I'll drive you.

SHE   You sure?

HE   Yeah I just have to find my keys. I put them somewhere. Listen, uh, how'd you like to have a drink? I thought we could talk.

SHE   (*yawning*) A little drink.

HE   You know, I put them somewhere. I just don't know where they are.

HE finds them in his coat pocket.

HE   Oh, I'm getting old.

SHE   You OK to drive?

HE   Yeah.

SHE leaves. HE takes a last look.

HE follows her.

SHE comes back.

SHE   I forgot something.

SHE picks up a rough clay mug with "#1 Dad" painted on it.

HE   Oh listen that reminds me. Tomorrow morning can we meet here, like first thing?

SHE   Sure, and then can you take me to the airport?

HE   Airport, what are you talking about?

SHE   My flight is – well, my flight isn't 'til 2:30. I could go back to the hotel.

HE   I thought you were staying a few more days.

SHE   No I'm not, I'm sure I told you.

HE   No you didn't.

SHE   I did.

HE   No. You didn't.

SHE   I'm sorry, I just assumed you knew.

HE   How could you assume?

SHE   Because it's the end of Shiva and I've got to get home.

HE   But there's lots left to do, there's a huge amount of stuff to do. I've been putting it off during Shiva but it's gotta get done now.

SHE   Well does it all have to get down right now?

HE   Well yeah some of it does. Some of it has to be done in the next few days.

SHE   Well, I'll go home and we can talk about it over the phone.

HE   But some of it has to be done here. I thought we could, you know, kinda share, doing it together. (*beat*) I've got a whole bunch of stuff on my plate, it's going to be hard for me to do this all by myself.

SHE   I'm not asking you to do it all by yourself.

HE   It's just–

SHE   I'm not implying you should do it all by yourself.

HE   It's just that it's a bit of a shock. Can we sit down for a second please?

> *SHE stares at him. Pause.*

> *Quick transition. HE removes his jacket and SHE whips off her scarf and they cross downstage. They address an unseen judge at various stages of their lives.*

> *As young kids.*

SHE   He looked at my fish!

HE   She was making that sound! (*SHE does.*) See!

SHE   He says I have monkey arms!

HE   She does have monkey arms and she keeps hitting me with her disgusting monkey arms!

> *SHE hits him with her monkey arms.*

Ow! See!

> *As young adults.*

SHE   We always have to do things his way, I mean always!

HE   She always has to be the centre of attention.

> *As pre-teens.*

SHE   He's handsome, and a good hockey player – but he stinks!

HE   And she comes into my room without knocking and she takes all my comic books and she doesn't put them back!

> *As adults.*

SHE   I can tell he's always seeking my approval, because, frankly he lives his life in a way that is less interesting than he could, and then he starts judging me, and I do just fine thanks for asking!

HE   She really is a very interesting person, it's just that sometimes she can't help herself from saying the wrong thing at the wrong time and basically she just doesn't know when to shut up!

> *As teenager.*

SHE   He took up all my space in the car and then he farted and left it there! And then he scratches his ass and he puts his fingers in my hair!

> *As middle-aged adults.*

HE   When the going gets tough, she takes off.

SHE   I take care of everything and I don't say a word and the minute he lifts a finger, we all have to bow down.

> *As teens.*

HE   ...and she always has to have like these new jeans or she always has to have like those new jeans and it doesn't even matter like which new jeans she has because her ass is still like 8 feet wide!

SHE   –and he stole all my change out of my sock drawer and I know it was him because I arrange my socks in an exact certain way and after, I put more in to test him and he stole that too!

As seniors.

HE   Maybe I'm a little slow, but I've finally come to
            realize... you can't change a person.

SHE   Well, you can't change.

They laugh.

As adults.

They face the audience with their backs to each other.

HE   (*simultaneous*) I'm really worried about her.

SHE   (*simultaneous*) I'm really worried about him.

They look at each other.

SHE   (*simultaneous*) He is not happy, and he thinks he has
            to follow this path that just leads to disappointment –
            I mean, live your life!

HE   (*simultaneous*) If she keeps on going in this way she
            won't have anything saved for her retirement, I
            mean, she can't work forever, what's she gonna do?

They nod to each other and have a little laugh.

HE &
SHE   S/He has terrible taste in women.

SHE gasps. SHE hits him.

As little kids.

HE   Ow.

SHE   He hit me first!

HE   She wrecked my plasticine.

BOTH   MOMMY!!!

As adult.

HE   The banal details of life are too petty for her to deal with.

As teens.

HE stomps on her foot.

SHE   You let him get away with murder!!

BOTH   DAD!

HE   –and she cries for no reason–

SHE does a fake laugh.

–and she has this fake laugh and she acts like this big environmentalist but she uses 80 gallons of water a day, and she *lies (her next speech starts here)* and then she convinces herself that she's not lying so she believes her lies so then she has to tell more lies to prove that she's right, and of course she's always got to be right! And meanwhile her room is full of plastic containers of junk food and now you say I can't go out until I clean up *my* room!!

SHE   –and he has to have those stupid shoes he wears on his stupid feet that look stupid on him because he can't play basketball because he's a shrimp!! And you buy him all this hockey equipment and now you're saying you can't afford to buy me one pair of plat- form shoes to wear to my party!!

BOTH   IT'S! NOT! FAIRRR!!!!

The lights change.

DANCE OF SIBS – 1

*They slowly turn and transform into adults. They see
each other, open their arms to each other in greeting
and say:*

BOTH   Hey.

*They dance a dance of sibling rivalry, employing
movements and gestures which will be echoed in later
scenes. They come together, clasp hands, and do a ritu-
alized cheek kiss, on both cheeks. SHE throws his arms
up in the air and tickles his belly. They laugh like kids.
HE drops his arms onto her shoulders like a wrestler,
SHE swings her arms onto his shoulders, HE shrugs
her arms off and slams his arms onto her shoulders.
SHE gasps and looks out as if seeing something in the
audience. HE turns to see it. SHE kicks him in the ass.
HE pushes her away and then grabs her arm and they
do a little swing dance which ends with her initiating
a competitive game where they each have arms
outstretched and attempt to touch each other, and
try to block each other. SHE ends it by touching his
chest with her finger. HE looks down and she flicks
him under the nose.*

SHE   Doink.

*HE hits her in the arm. They gasp! SHE puts her
hands out and they play the hand slap game. SHE
slaps him a few times, then misses. They switch. HE
slaps her gleefully a few times, then misses. SHE turns
and puts her arms up in victory, with her back to him.
SHE falls backwards, HE catches her. SHE relaxes in
his arms as if drunk, and turns to try and kiss his
cheek. HE shrugs her away with his shoulder and
leaves her standing alone, back to the audience.*

*SHE is left alone, in a spot. As the following parental
voices start, she becomes a two and a half year old,
basking in her parents' attention.*

VOICE
OVER   –Who's my baby?
–Who's Daddy's girl?
–Who's my beautiful girl?
–Who's my clever girl?
–Who's my (*babytalk gobbledygook*)?
–Who's the best baby in the whole wide world?
–Who's the one I love?
–Who's Mommy's girl?
–(*babytalk gobbledygook*)

(*the "Dad"*) Hey.... Hey.... Guess what? You have...
a brand... new... baby... brother!

> *SHE is shocked, then disappointed, then upset and*
> *mad.*

SHE   I thought it was a girl!

> *A baby is discovered on stage, gurgling, with a soother*
> *in his mouth. SHE squats on her haunches looking at*
> *him, fascinated. SHE plays peek-a-boo. HE laughs.*
> *SHE is thrilled, looks to the unseen judge and laughs.*
> *SHE does it again, bigger. HE laughs more. SHE*
> *laughs more. SHE does it again, too loudly. Suddenly*
> *HE cries and SHE doesn't know why. SHE reacts by*
> *smothering him with her body.*

> *Blackout.*

> *HE is sitting up. SHE dresses him like a girl. SHE*
> *introduces him to imaginary people.*

SHE   Hi, Mr. Fireman. This is my new baby sister, Cindy.

> *SHE gets him up and drags him and skips over*
> *somewhere else.*

SHE   Hi, Mr. Chinese Grocery lady. This is my new baby
sister, Cindy. Say hi Cindy.

HE   Henh.

SHE   Hi.

HE   Henh.

SHE   Hi!

> *SHE waves at him, HE tries to wave at her.*

Dance!!

> *They dance.*

> *Transition. They return to the first scene of the play.*

HE   I just thought... that because there's a whole bunch of stuff to do, and because some of it is time sensitive, right?

> *HE takes a pack of cigarettes out of his jacket pocket. SHE watches.*

Some of it has to be done right now. Well, some of it is legal stuff, right? Lawyer stuff, the death certificate, getting the will probated–

> *SHE sighs heavily as HE begins to light his cigarette. HE puts the cigarette away.*

–that kind of stuff, right?

SHE   Right, but I don't have to just sit here in the city, I don't have to just sit here, some of these things just happen–

HE   No they have to be dealt–

SHE   –right?

HE   –somebody has to be in charge. Somebody has to make sure that they're done, right?

SHE   Right. And you don't want to do it.

HE   Well – I–

SHE   Well, let's do it long distance.

HE   No uh–

SHE   You know what, I'll do it? Give me the number–

HE   Excuse me–

SHE   –of – I'll get the number from the lawyer and I'll just handle it all long distance. You don't have to do it. I understand, you're busy.

> *Lights change and they are now little kids.*

SHE   Do you want to play with plasticine?

HE   Yeah.

SHE   Do you know where my plasticine is?

HE   Yeah.

SHE   It's in my room. In my closet! GO! Go! Go go go go go go go go go go!

> *HE runs up the stairs to her room and gets it.*

> *They play for a few seconds. SHE pretends to sneeze plasticine out her nose. HE laughs. SHE watches him.*

What are you making? A snake? A bone?

HE   Mommy.

SHE   I'm making mommy too. Isn't mine good?

HE   Yeah.

SHE   Yours is good... too.

> *They work a bit.*

SHE   Hey! Can you get me a drink?

HE   Yeah.

SHE   Go! go go go go go go go go go go!

> *HE runs off to get it but is gone a long while. After a pause, SHE yells.*

SHE   Where are you?

HE   In the kitchen!

SHE   Come here with the drink!

HE   (*beat*) Oh yeah!

> *HE does, they keep working.*

SHE   Does Mommy have hair?

HE   No.

SHE   Yes, she does. Do you know where the wool is?!

HE   Yeah.

SHE   Go! go go go go go!

> *HE runs to go get it. SHE meanwhile has fixed his plasticine. HE comes back with some wool.*

SHE   Oh no, I meant the yellow yarn!

> *HE sees his "mommy." HE is upset.*

SHE   I fixed it. Your mommy looked like a bug.

> *HE wrecks both of their plasticine.*

SHE   What are you doing?! You ruin everything!

> *SHE hits him. HE cries.*

SHE   I'm never playing with you again!

BOTH   Mommy!

> *They stomp off to their rooms, and address the unseen judge.*

Mommy!

> *Transition.*
> *They greet each other. They are young adults.*

Heeeey.

> *They cross to greet each other.*

SHE   Hey Stinky!!!

HE   Pigbag!

SHE   Happy Pesach!

HE   Yeah happy Passover to you too. Hey, come here.

> *They go to her "room."*

Tah dah!

SHE   I see you wasted no time getting into my room.

HE   Well it's a lot bigger than my old room. Oh, by the way, I put all your stuff in the basement.

SHE   (*beat*) Did you wrap my glass ducks?

HE   Yes.

SHE   Did you label the boxes?

HE   Well, Dad did.

SHE   Oh of course, alphabetically I bet.

> *They laugh.*

Look at you! Look how big you are!

HE   Thanks. You too.

SHE   (*beat*) Thanks...

HE   So, how's college?

SHE   Boring. My professors are boring. The courses are boring. The students are boring. They've all lived such sheltered lives! Let me give you some advice. Do not go straight to university. Take a year or two off.

HE   I'm going to.

SHE   You are!? What are you going to do? Travel? Europe? Israel? Or are you still not Jewish? I see you're wearing a Kipa, at least.

HE   I'm still an atheist. I just don't want to hurt Boubi's feelings.

SHE   You could trek to Everest base camp in Nepal. They'll take you up to like 17,000 feet. That's what I'd do. Or India!

HE   I got a job. A full-time job.

SHE   Great. Where?

HE   At the mall. The Triple S? (*beat*) Super Sports Store?

SHE   Ohh. Doing what?

HE   Selling sports equipment. The pay's really good. Soon I'll be able to move out and... I'm going to get a car!

SHE   Good for you! Oh. Listen, Mom told me about the hockey exam.

HE   Try-out. It's no big deal.

SHE   Sure it's a big deal. You must have been really disappointed.

HE   I just blew it, that's all.

SHE   That's not all. Come on. You can tell me.

HE   (*beat*) Well, I had a bad game, and–

SHE   Oh God I know what you mean! I presented my first short film in film class and everybody laughed and it wasn't a comedy!

HE   Anyway, the scout told the coach I was too small.

        SHE hits him.

SHE   You're not too small!

HE   I am. Anyway, who cares. It's just hockey.

        SHE hits him.

SHE   But you love hockey.

HE   I told you it doesn't matter.

        SHE hits him.

SHE   Sure it matters.

HE   I don't want to talk about it.

        Pause. HE turns away. SHE sits, mystified.

SHE   The one good course I'm taking is Ancient Hebraic Studies. It's where you study the bible in the original Hebrew. It's actually very interesting. It's like everything we were taught about the Bible is like totally... wrong! Like with Cain and Abel, for example, what actually happened was that God preferred Abel's offering to Cain's. And then it says about Cain, "Vayeeflooh panav" which means, "And it fell, his face." And God says to Cain "Why is your face falling, if you would have given me as good an offering as your brother Abel's, I would have preferred yours too." So Cain goes off, gets an AK-47, kills his brother! I mean, they were *set up* to fight. That's what's going on with all these civil wars, and like between the Arabs and the Jews, and... (*beat*) We should have some good long talks while I'm here.

HE   Are you stoned?

SHE   I wish. I don't know if I can handle Uncle Joey's jokes if my mind is still in this dimension.

HE   Well, how would you like to go for a walk with me and my friend "Doobie"?

> *HE takes a joint out of his pocket.*

> *SHE takes one out as well.*

SHE   If I can bring my friend "Mary Jane."

> *They laugh and morph into kids laughing. SHE smacks him on the arm.*

SHE   You're it!

> *HE chases her. They play tag. Finally HE smacks her arm.*

HE   You're it!

> *SHE smacks him back immediately.*

SHE   You're it!

HE   No touchbacks!

SHE   Yes touchbacks. Stamped it.

HE   You can't do that! You can't change the rules!

SHE   Yes I can! Because I am Ruler of the Universe and everything I say goes and nothing you say goes and you are it! Stamped it! Stamped it! Stamped it!

HE   Mom!

SHE   Mom!

HE   Stop it!

SHE   Stop it!

HE   Stop copying me.

SHE   Stop copying me!

HE   Mom, she's copying me!

SHE   Mom, she's copying me!

> *HE hits her. THEY gasp. SHE runs after him. HE
> falls to the ground, and SHE straddles him.*

SHE   Say it! Say it!

HE   No!

> *SHE starts to spit.*

SHE   Who's your boss!

HE   No one!

SHE   (*slapping his face*) You lie you lie you lie! Who's your
                boss?!

HE   You are.

SHE   What are you?

HE   I'm me!

SHE   (*slapping his face*) You lie you lie you lie! What are
                you?!

HE   Your slave.

SHE   I can't hear you.

HE   YOUR SLAVE!

SHE	That's right. (*kisses him*) What a good boy! (*SHE jumps up*.) You're it! Come on. Play.
HE	I'm not playing with you.
SHE	Suck!
HE	I'm gonna go tell Mommy. You're gonna be in big trouble.
SHE	(*imitating Mom for his benefit*) You're gonna be in big trouble, young man! You play nicely with your baby brother, young lady.
HE	(*reluctantly laughing*) That's Mommy!
SHE	(*SHE looks for mom and laughs evilly.*) You two go into your very own rooms and have a big breath.
HE	You wait until your Father gets home. (*as father*) I'll give you something to–
BOTH	–really cry about.
SHE	You two go downstairs and pick up all your toys.
HE	Pick up your poo!
SHE	Pick up your poo, and eat it like pudding, young man!
HE	Stop it I have to pee!
SHE	Put your pee on your poo and have a poopudding popsicle young man!
HE	Stop it. I have to pee.
SHE	Don't pee!
HE	Don't do that.
SHE	Pssss.

HE   Stop it!

SHE   Pss psss pssss.

HE   No no stop stop. (*silent beat*) Oh no!! I peed! / / I peed!

        // *indicates when they overlap.*

SHE   You peed! You peed! *I* made you pee!!

        SHE throws her arms up, victorious

        Her laugh becomes the laugh of a drunk teen. SHE turns and starts to walk to the door, upstage.

SHE   You peed. I made you pee, mister.

        SHE slips and sinks to the ground, nauseous.

        HE enters.

HE   Shh. You'll wake up Mom and Dad.

SHE   You peed. I made you pee.

HE   That's good. Now, come on, let's get you upstairs.

        HE tries to pick her up.

SHE   You smell like... potatoes.

HE   We've got to get you upstairs before Mom and Dad hear.

SHE   No! I want to sleep here.

        SHE sinks to the floor, face down.

HE   You can't. They'll find you like this again. You know, you've got to stop doing this.

SHE   Shutup! (*laughing*) You suck-up stupid little brat.

HE   Fine. I'll just leave you here.

      HE leaves, SHE lies there, whimpering.

SHE   Nooo, don't leave me, ohh.

      Frustrated, HE comes back and turns her over with his foot. SHE giggles.

HE   What are you trying to prove?

      HE lifts her in a fireman's lift.

SHE   Do you have a girlfriend?

HE   None of your business.... Do you have a boyfriend?

SHE   None of *your* business.

HE   God. You're disgusting.

SHE   *You're* disgusting.

HE   You're acting like a pigbag.

SHE   *You* are acting like a fucking pigbag.

      SHE spirals down his body onto the floor again.

HE   Shh! You know, if they see you like this again you'll be grounded for the rest of your life!

      SHE sneaks through his legs and stands behind him.

SHE   Since when do you care?

HE   Didn't you say you were going to be at Sheryl's tonight, you liar?

SHE   I might as well lie. I get blamed for everything. You never get blamed for anything!

HE   That's 'cause I never do anything!

SHE	Who broke the Elf paperweight?!
HE	Who pushed me?
SHE	(*SHE smiles.*) I never said I'd be "at Sheryl's" I said I'd be "with Sheryl."
HE	Well Sheryl called here looking for you.
SHE	Oh shit!
HE	I tried to cover for you, but it all sounded pretty lame to me.
SHE	I always covered for you and everybody believed me. Why doesn't anybody believe me anymore?!
HE	Um, because you lie all the time?
SHE	Well, I wouldn't have to lie all the time if people would just trust me!
HE	Shh. Do you want to get us both in trouble?!

> *HE puts his hand over her mouth. SHE bites his hand.*

	Ow!
SHE	Hey! Where's my hat?!
HE	Get up those fucking stairs this fucking second or I'll fucking pound your fucking face in!
SHE	I love you.
HE	Yeah, whatever.

> *HE starts to drag her away. SHE stops them.*

SHE	Spinning.
HE	Are you going to barf?
SHE	No.

       They continue. SHE stops.

SHE   Why are you being so nice to me?

HE   Believe me, you're gonna owe me big time. Now, let's go.

SHE   Uh oh.

HE   What?

       SHE barfs on him.

HE   Ewww!!

       SHE continues a gagging noise that turns into hyperventilating kid crying. His shirt wiping turns into a little kid crying.

       SHE is packing a small suitcase with clothes and food.

       HE stands there and watches. HE is crying.

SHE   They hate me! I'm going!! They'll be sorry when I'm gone away!

HE   Where are you going?

SHE   Far a-way!

HE   Don't go. I don't want you to go!

SHE   I have to. I'm going.

HE   Don't go. Please don't go.

       SHE exits. HE cries, inconsolable. SHE watches him for a moment in the doorway.

SHE   Oĸ. Shh Shh. I won't go. I'll stay. Because of you.... But next time... I'm going.

       They slowly transform to adults.

They are back in that first scene.

HE   No. Some of it can't be done long distance. Like
     you have to open up a bank account, and we have
     to do that at Dad's old bank. And because we're
     co-executers of the estate, that means we have to be
     co-signers of the account. And so–

SHE I wish you would have told me all this, this week.

HE   Well, we were sitting Shiva, for god's sake.

SHE Well I could have taken an afternoon off and gone
     and done this.

HE   But that's not what Shiva's about. When you sit
     Shiva, you sit Shiva. You don't do that. And then so
     I thought like we would sit Shiva and then like next
     week, or starting tomorrow or whenever–

SHE But you work here and you live here, and I can't do
     that.

HE   I understand that.

SHE You understand that?

HE   I do understand that.

DANCE OF SIBS 2

*They start warily, and repeat the beginning portion of
the first Dance of Sibs. When they get to the part
where SHE tries to kick him in the ass, HE catches her
before SHE can kick him and swings her off into the
swing dance. They extend the swing dance portion,
with high "teen" energy. They end by coming together,
face to face. They pause, freaked out at their proximity,
and then swing each other off into their own rooms.*

*SHE gets her guitar. Beat. HE looks at her. SHE makes
faces at him.*

SHE   What?!

HE   Nothing.

> *Lights change.*

> *This is his fantasy rehearsal of how HE would ask her for advice. HE and SHE face the audience.*

HE   Can I ask you a question?

SHE   I don't know, can you?

HE   There's this dance tonight, and I wanted to know, if you're slow dancing with a girl is it OK–

SHE   Yuck! Ick! Gross! Disgusting!

> *HE waves away that attempt and tries another.*

HE   Can I ask you a question?

SHE   Sure.

HE   Say, hypothetically, I was slow dancing with a girl–

SHE   Who?!

HE   Well, it doesn't matter who.

SHE   Rochelle?

HE   No, not Rochelle.

SHE   Oooh, Rochelle. Rochellllle!

> *HE waves away that attempt and tries another.*

HE   I have this friend–

SHE   You do?

HE   Yes.

SHE   Oh.

HE   And he wanted me to ask you–

SHE   Who?

HE   Uh... Todd.

SHE   Yich.

HE   Yeah. Well, he wanted me to ask you, if he's slow dancing with a girl–

SHE   Who?!

HE   Oh, I can't say. I promised.

SHE   Rochelle?

HE   No! Todd doesn't like Rochelle.

SHE   No, but Rochelle likes Todd...

> *HE waves away that attempt and tries another. Faster.*

HE   Can I ask you a question!?

SHE   Yes!

HE   Todd wanted me to ask you if he's slow dancing with a girl, is it OK if I kiss him!?

SHE   I think you should kiss him.

> *HE waves away that attempt and lights return to normal. HE turns and looks at her.*
>
> *Pause.*

SHE   What?

HE   Nothing.

> *Pause. HE goes to work putting tape on his hockey stick. SHE watches him.*

SHE Are you going to that dance tonight?

HE What dance?

SHE (*mocking*) Uh, what dance.

HE Yeah.

SHE Well, what are you gonna wear?

HE What I always wear.

SHE Oh no. You're not.

HE Why not?

SHE Because you look like a jock.

HE I am a jock.

SHE I know, but you smell like a jock. I mean, literally. A jock. And your shoes stink, and your socks reek, and your pants smell like skid marks and stale farts and you stink like BO, and you have this stink coming off you, it's like a stinky rank stank, skunky funky funk stinky stink stank rank skank skanky stinkudee skunk stank! (*beat*) I mean you really do smell–

HE Alright! Ok!

> *Pause. SHE looks at him.*

SHE Hey, stinky,

HE What?

SHE Can I ask you a question?

HE (*suspiciously*) What?

SHE About... hockey.

HE   Why?

SHE   Because, I need to know about offside.

HE   Why?

SHE   Because – I'm doing a school project on offside!

HE   Yeah. Why?

SHE   Because! I'm going to a hockey game with...
           somebody! and I need to know about offside –
           what is offside!

HE   With who?

SHE   No way!

HE   OK, five bucks.

           *HE takes a piece of paper and starts writing
           something.*

SHE   What?! I give you advice all the time for free! And I'm
           so nice.

HE   Sure, Stinky. Five bucks.

           *HE starts to cross into her room, SHE speaks in a
           pleading baby voice.*

SHE   Please...

HE   Six.

SHE   Come on...

HE   Seven.

SHE   You're so handsome and nice...

HE   Eight.

SHE   Alright! Five bucks!

> *HE holds out the paper. It is an IOU.*

HE   Sign here.

> *SHE spins him around and uses his back to sign the IOU, ending with three hard pokes.*

Ow. (*HE draws.*) OK. Here's the rink, right? And here are the goals. Here are the lines. Now, the most important thing to remember about offside is that the puck has to be the first thing that crosses the other team's blue line. Right? So, if two guys are skating into the other team's zone, the guy who doesn't have the puck can't cross the blue line before the guy who does have the puck. Well, for that matter, if you have the puck and skate in backwards over the blue line, that also would be offside–

> *SHE has been listening, uncomprehending, and getting frustrated.*

> *Lights change, they are adults, back to the first scene. SHE is behind him, frustrated. HE faces the audience, for the whole scene, as if talking to her.*

HE   So, all I would like if possible is for you to stay a few more days now, we can get started on it, and then you can go back home–

SHE   I need to get home now.

HE   Well, what's the soonest you can get back?

SHE   I don't know.

HE   You don't know?

SHE   No I don't know because this is all new to me. This is all new information// to me

HE   Well, this is all new to me too, this is all new information to me that you're leaving.

SHE   But you do know that I don't live in this city?

HE   Of course I do, but as far as I knew you were staying until Thursday. That's that last information I heard.

SHE   Where'd you get that information?

HE   You.

           Beat.

SHE   I don't think so. OK.

           Back to previous scene.

HE   OK. So that's the two-line-pass type of offside. Well, do you have any questions?

SHE   Yes! Do you think it's possible...

HE   Yeah?

SHE   –that you are actually... (*as an alien*) an alien? (*SHE pretends to shoot him with a laser gun.*) Zot. Zot.

           HE starts to leave.

HE   Five bucks.

SHE   Zot.

           HE leaves. SHE sticks her head out the door and mocks him.

SHE   (*under her breath*) Five bucks.

           HE looks back but SHE's gone. HE gives her the finger. SHE almost catches him. They go to their rooms. SHE turns on music.

           HE turns on his music. They have a music blasting war, trying to drown each other out. They end by stamping toward each other menacingly, as monsters.

           Transition.

> *They greet each other as adults, with arms open.*

BOTH   Heeeyyy!

HE   Good to see you!

SHE   Happy Pesach. (*SHE scratches his goatee.*) What's this? (*like a goat*) Baaaah.

HE   Oh, you're so skinny.

SHE   Aw, come on.

HE   So, I guess you're still smoking?

SHE   Obviously, you?

HE   Yeah. Come on.

> *HE ushers her into her old "room."*

HE   So. What do you think of the panelling?

SHE   Ich. Well, Dad finally got his den.

HE   Yeah. Well, you know, the paint never really covered the–

SHE   Hole!

HE   Yeah, when you put my head // through the wall.

SHE   Where your head went through the wall!

> *SHE laughs at the memory. HE does not. Beat.*
>
> *They go to the "living room."*

So you're definitely not going back to school?

HE   Why bother?

SHE   How's your new job?

HE   Great. Great.

SHE   Yeah?

HE   Yeah, you know, I think there's a real future for me there.

SHE   Great.

HE   They really value me there.

SHE   Really?

HE   Yeah. Everyday I go in there and there's new challenges–

SHE   So you're happy?

HE   I look forward to going in–

SHE   Wonderful

HE   –every day and–

              Reality Bubble – as kids. SHE slaps his face.

SHE   You lie you lie you lie!

              Back to adults.

HE   –every day it's fun and creative and–

SHE   Wonderful.

HE   Yeah.

SHE   Yeah.

              Beat.

              So how's Rochelle?

HE   (*conspiratorially*) Well, we haven't said anything to Mom or Dad yet, but... we're moving in together.

SHE   Wow! That's... huge!

HE   Yeah.

SHE   Congratulations.

HE   Thank you.

SHE   You'll have to tell me all about it sometime.

         Beat.

HE   OK. So, what about you? How's your love life?

SHE   Oh you know, no one special.

HE   Oh, so you're just sleeping around like a pigbag?

         Beat. SHE eyes him and comes closer.

SHE   Does Rochelle mind that... smell?

HE   She loves it.

SHE   Yich.

         They sit.

HE   And how's work?

SHE   Yeah!

HE   Are you working?

SHE   Yeah.

HE   Oh!

SHE   You know...

HE   Uh huh?

SHE   Yeah.

HE waits.

It's like... yeah.

HE Uh huh.

HE nods.

SHE Yeah. Lots on the go. Still trying to stay in the creative end. Don't want to get all corporate.

HE Oh sure.

HE nods.

SHE Lots of irons in lots of fires...

HE Mhm.

SHE Pretty soon one of them's going to catch on and I'll make a million bucks!

HE (*laughing*) Yeah, right.

SHE What's that supposed to mean?

HE Nothing. I'm agreeing with you.

SHE (*imitating him exactly*) "Yeah right."

HE starts to go.

HE Fine.

SHE Fine.

HE Stop that.

SHE Stop that.

Reality Bubble – they become little kids.

HE Stop copying me.

SHE Stop copying me.

HE Mom she's copying me!

SHE Mom she's copying me!

> *HE smacks her. They gasp. Back to adults.*

SHE Hey.

HE Yeah?

SHE Did you bring the dessert?

HE Was I supposed to?

SHE That's OK. I brought it.

> *SHE pats his face, and leaves.*

> *Transition. HE fumes.*

> *They become kids. HE takes a swing at her, misses. SHE easily holds him at arm's distance by his head. HE swings wildly, not connecting. SHE laughs. HE gets more and more frustrated. SHE pushes him away. HE charges her, SHE does a matador-like evasion. HE comes at her again. SHE side-steps him (like opening a door). HE hits her. SHE laughs. HE hits her again. SHE laughs again. SHE chases him, playing like she's going to kiss him. HE runs to his room, slamming his door.*

> *HE fantasizes an elaborate murder of her. SHE stands apart from him facing downstage. HE mimes strangling, snapping her neck, opening up her chest, ripping out her heart, biting it off, and throwing it to the ground and stamping on it until it stops beating. SHE goes through the motions as if he was really doing it to her. Beat.*

HE I wish I had a brother! (*SHE is lying prone.*) I really really need a brother. I know what he looks like.

*The lights change. SHE gets up and becomes his
fantasy brother – embodying all his actions and
descriptions.*

He's older than her, and he's tall, and he's strong,
with big muscles, and short hair, and a cool smile!
And he smiles only at me, never at her. And if she
smiles at him, he beats her up. And we're a team, him
and me, and she can never ever be on our team or
make us get mad at each other or break us up for
even a single second. And we play football together.
And he shows me how to throw a perfect spiral.
(*does*) Cool! And he helps me. He helps me with my
homework... (*does*) ...thanks... and he tells me stuff
about life. (*SHE whispers in his ear and makes a motion
that implies the "facts of life".*) WOW! And he never
ever beats me up. (*SHE does beat him up.*) Well, just
when we're having fun. And everything is perfect!
It's just me and my brother.

*They laugh gleefully together. SHE turns, smiles at
someone else and walks off. HE calls after her.*

HE   Hey, where're you goin'? Can I come...? Hey, wait up!
(*SHE is gone.*) Okay, catch you later.

The lights change.

HE works on his hockey stick.

*SHE is no longer the brother, but herself as a young
teen. SHE looks at him.*

SHE   Can I ask you something?

HE   (*suspiciously*) What?

SHE   Can you come here for a second? Can you sit over
here, please?

HE does.

OK. Say you don't know me. And say you saw me
walking on the street – could you look straight ahead

please? Would you think I was cool or a loser?
Straight ahead, please.

SHE walks.

HE   ...Cool.

SHE   Yeah?

HE   Yeah.

SHE   OK, say you don't know me, and you just saw me—
look straight ahead—walking down the street, would
you think I had a walk of self-confidence or not?
Straight ahead, thank you.

SHE walks.

HE   Self... self-confident.

SHE   Yeah? I think I'm ready.

*Suddenly SHE realizes SHE's got the wrong hair
ribbon on.*

Where is my hair ribbon?

HE   In your hand?

SHE   No. Not this one, the red one. The one I just bought
today for tonight. I just bought it. Where is it? I can't
wear brown and green!

HE   Well, why don't you wear your hair down? It looks
OK–

SHE   I can't wear my hair *down*! Look at it! It's all flat and
it parts in the middle and I look like a loser!

HE   Why don't you ask Mom where it is–

SHE   (*exploding*) Because Mom doesn't know anything! and
she has the same horrible hair as I do and oh no!
(*SHE collapses to the floor.*) nobody's going to dance

with me again! You're not helping me!! Leave me alone!! Leave me alone!!

> *SHE hits him with her monkey arms and stomps off to her room, hysterically sobbing.*

> *Beat.*

HE   What did I do?

> *HE goes to his room. SHE goes and gets her guitar and begins strumming a minor chord. SHE strums and sings a poem.*

SHE   Darkness
Darkne-hess
(*very low*) Darkness.
Darkness is every-where...

> *There is noise from his room. SHE yells at him.*

Can you please... shutup!
Darkness is like self-confidence. It sucks in everything and gives nothing away...

> *SHE stops singing, and just talks to the audience.*

I am psycho. I am absolutely 100% psycho. How to stop being a complete psychopath and be normal?!

> *SHE strums again, more forcefully.*

Stop watching TV
Get a boyfriend!
Stop bothering my baby brother.

> *HE's making more noise in his room. SHE yells for his benefit.*

I HATE him! It's my fault he's such an ASSHOLE. I'm not nice to him.

> *SHE starts to strum and make up a folk rant. HE tiptoes to her door and eavesdrops.*

And yesterday on the Cummer 42 bus, a man was sitting across from me and he was picking his nose! and eating it! And he was in his forties!! And then there was a lawn statue that was of a black person and that just made me sick. And I just wanted to ask god himself—or herself—why!

HE is now standing in her doorway and he can't contain a muffled guffaw. SHE pauses, thinking SHE hears something. Beat of silence. SHE resumes as before.

Why! The holocaust had to happen and why do all the people die, and why do the animals suffer so much in the world, they didn't do anything! And please don't let me hurt my brother, because it would be so easy.

HE makes a noise.

HE   Pffff.

SHE jumps up and screams at a pitch that would break glass.

SHE   GET OUT OF MY ROOOOOOM!!!

HE runs away. SHE recovers.

Beat.

HE starts to go to the living room. SHE stops him.

Hey.

HE   What?

SHE   Where are you going?

HE   Downstairs.

SHE   What are you going to do? Watch the hockey game?

HE   Yeah.

SHE   Are we playing?

HE   Yeah.

SHE   Who're we playing?

HE   Pittsburgh.

SHE   Oohhhh.

> *HE starts to go again.*

Give me a kiss.

HE   What?

SHE   Give me a kiss.

HE   Why?

SHE   What if one of us dies in our sleep tonight?! Give me a kiss!!

> *HE comes over reluctantly. SHE gives him one, SHE holds him in place.*

SHE   I love you!

HE   Yeah, whatever.

> *HE tries to leave.*

SHE   Give me one.

> *HE reluctantly does.*

SHE   What a good boy! Good.

> *SHE turns away. HE looks at her back with total disbelief. SHE waits.*

Get... out.

> *SHE rolls her eyes.*

HE   What a psycho.

          *SHE gasps, hurt. HE smiles and leaves. SHE turns to
          him.*

          Transition. They are now slightly older teenagers.

SHE   Hey.

HE   What?

SHE   Where are you going?

HE   Downstairs.

SHE   No you're not.

HE   Yes I am.

SHE   No you are not.

HE   Yes I am!

SHE   No, you're not! Put on a Kipa.

HE   I'm sorry, but I don't believe in God.

SHE   Ach! Put on a Kipa and get dressed nice, and stop
          yelling! Do you want to get us both in trouble?!

HE   What are you, I've already got a mother thank you
          very much. Since when do you care?

SHE   Since I care. And maybe when you grow up, and you
          start thinking about people besides yourself, you'll
          realize you don't say things like that!

HE   What, lightning's going to strike?

SHE   We are Jews. Jews celebrate Pesach. Just because Mr.
          Hockey Star–

HE   Here we go. Ms. Zionism. I'm not saying I'm not
          Jewish.

SHE	Uh, a Jew who doesn't believe in god!?
HE	Yes.
SHE	Uh, that's ridiculous!
HE	Karl Marx, Sigmund Freud, Leon Trotsky... Groucho Marx!
SHE	Ok fine, you don't believe in God, give back all your Bar Mitzva presents! Give them all back. And all that money. Give them to me! I didn't get any money! You don't believe, give it all back!
HE	I believed in it then, I don't now.
SHE	Oh god! Last year you were a vegetarian–
HE	I'm still a vegetarian.
SHE	Is chopped liver a vegetable?
HE	I am not going to be a hypocrite.

> *Doorbell rings. HE starts to leave, SHE grabs his arm and spins him around.*

SHE	You are not going down there dressed like that, and smelling like BO on Pesach!
HE	I just had a shower!
SHE	Well, it didn't take!! And you are not telling Boubi there is no god!
HE	I will if she asks me.
SHE	You want her to ask you!!

> *Doorbell – parents voices.*

HE	You know, you act all high and mighty and mean-while you're coming home drunk every / / second night.

SHE   I wouldn't have to get drunk if I didn't have a brother// like you!

HE   Yeah, you know what it's like// being your brother

SHE   Do you know what it's like being your sister?!

HE   Everybody laughs at you// behind your back–

SHE   Everybody thinks you're stupid!!

HE   –because you can't get a boyfriend!!!

SHE gasps.

Ah, fuck you.

HE starts to leave. SHE grabs him. They fight. Big. It ends with him punching her in the stomach, hard. SHE is hurt, doubled over in pain.

Pause.

Are you OK?

HE reaches out to her. SHE slaps his hand away. SHE starts to go, turn. They stare at each other.

DANCE OF SIBS - 3

HE tries to encourage her to join in, by opening his arms to her. SHE comes over slowly, and gently, grudgingly, but politely they kiss. They dance and she starts to loosen up. HE twirls her, SHE spins, HE is gone.

Transition.

They are adults. Older than the previous Pesach – late twenties.

BOTH   Hey!

HE   Happy Pesach.

SHE   To you too.

HE   Oh, you are so skinny.

SHE   Yeah don't say anything to Mom and Dad about it though, you know how they get.

HE   Oh. Sure. So you're still smoking?

SHE   Obviously. You?

HE   I quit.

SHE   Wow! Great! (*patting his gut*) So that's what all this is. It looks good on you, though.

HE   Hey Dad told me about your new contract. Mazel Tov.

SHE   No "Mazel" involved, Mr. Jewinhymer.

HE   So this is a full time thing?

SHE   Yeah.

HE   Uh huh.

SHE   Yeah.

HE   Mhm?

SHE   You know.

HE   Yeah?

SHE   Yeah. (*beat*) I make my own schedule, and I get to travel a lot. I still have to do some gofer-y things, but I get to meet filmmakers and chose their films!

HE   Wow.

SHE   Yeah. You know how I was just in Israel, right?

HE   Oh yes, I heard all about it.

SHE   Oh. Great. Well I got Mom and Dad this Menorah blessed by a Rabbi, who is also... a filmmaker!

HE   Oh.

SHE   Mom's looking at it right now.

HE   Well, how's Peter with all that travel?

SHE   Peter? He's fine.

HE   Won't it be a strain on your relationship?

SHE   Relationship? He's my roommate.

HE   Oh. I thought the two of you were... uh...

SHE   (*laughing*) Nooo. Peter's gay.

HE   Ohhh.

SHE   You have a problem with that?

HE   No. Do you?

SHE   No, of course not. Do you?

HE   No! (*beat*) Well, Mom and Dad think you're a couple.

SHE   They do?

HE   Yeah.

SHE   Is that what they said?

HE   Yeah.

SHE   What did they say?

HE   They said, "We think they're a couple."

SHE   And what did you say?

HE	I said I didn't know.
SHE	And they think we're living together?
HE	Well, you are living together.
SHE	And they're OK with that?
HE	In fact, I think they were kind of relieved.

Beat.

SHE	Do *you* think we'd be a good couple?
HE	Do you want to be a couple?
SHE	Well, he's gay.
HE	Yeah.
SHE	And you have a problem with that?!
HE	No!!
SHE	Not everyone wants to be married with kids you know.
HE	Yeah. (*beat*) So, are you gonna tell them?
SHE	No. Just let them think it. What's the big deal. OK?
HE	OK.

Long pause.

SHE	So, how's work?
HE	(*sarcastically*) Ha ha ha.
SHE	OK. And how's work?
HE	Didn't Dad tell you?
SHE	Dad doesn't tell me anything. You tell me what Dad wants to tell me.

HE   When you came in, just now, what did Dad say?

SHE   He said "What's that thing in your hair?"

HE   Hunh. There you go.

SHE   What?

HE   (*beat*) They let me go.

SHE   What?!

HE   Downsizing.

SHE   How could they do that? You were the best guy there! You... started that whole...

HE   Department.

SHE   –department thing!

SHE   Those bastards!

HE   Yeah well.

SHE   What did you do?

HE   Well, it was a bit of a shock, but... I've redone my resume, you know. I'm going for some interviews–

SHE   No no no. I mean what did you *do*. To get fired. What'd you do?

HE   Thank you for your support.

HE starts to go.

SHE   Your temper?

HE   Fuck you!

SHE   Where's Rochelle?

HE   We split up!

SHE   Ohhh...

> *HE goes.*

Yes!!

> *They become adults. SHE speaks as if to an audience at a wedding. HE gets ready in a mirror.*

First of all I would like to thank all the people who made it here from out of town: Uncle Joey from Mantawk Long Island, Auntie Rivka bat Ziporah hagalilee, from Kibbutz in Israel – oh and hello to the big table from South Africa here for Rochelle. I only wish my Bouba Bessie was here to see this blessed event. I'm sure she is smiling down on us, shepping nachas that one of us got married, and in a big downtown synagogue no less. I guess I'm off the hook.

> *SHE turns to him and they practice the Four Questions as children. SHE helps and gently prompts him through it.*

HE   Mah neeshtanah. Ha lylah hah...

SHE   Hahzeh.

HE   Hahzeh. Me Kohl Halaylot...

SHE   Sheh bekol..

HE   Sheh bekol halaylot anu ochlin hametz oooooo...

BOTH   MATZAH!

> *They laugh and SHE turns back to the wedding speech.*

SHE   I'd like to offer my new sister—I've always wanted a little sister—a word or two of advice. Firstly, the smell. You'll just have to get used to it. Believe me, we've tried everything. (*SHE tells the joke awkwardly, and then enjoys it.*) Secondly, Rochelle, as you know, when my brother sets his mind to something—or someone—he never lets go. Even if... he's wrong.

> *SHE turns as HE begins a speech. They are teens. It is his Bar Mitzvah speech. His voice occasionally breaks. SHE sits and watches proudly.*

HE I'd like to thank everybody for coming to my Bar Mitzvah. (*SHE applauds enthusiastically, and he gives her a look.*) Shh. For my D'var Torah I'd like to talk about my Parshah which is about the exodus of the Jews from Egypt. At Pesach, the Haggadah asks us to think as if we ourselves were slaves in Egypt. It also asks us to think of all those who might be enslaved today. And as my sister always says, you gotta question authority.

> *SHE looks out to the audience and shakes her head, shyly, denying she said that.*

HE So, I began thinking of all those people who we, as Jews, might be enslaving. (*beat*) Like, the Palestinians in Israel.

UNCLE JOEY (*the musician*) Oy.

HE Or the Falashas, the African Jews of Israel.

> *Mortified, SHE begins to leave and return to her downstage spot. HE is losing confidence.*

HE Or even people here at home.

> *They are back at the wedding. HE is enjoying her speech.*

SHE Oh, Rochelle. He gave my parents plenty to worry about: skating head first into a zamboni, making me chase him out of a tree fort, landing on his head, or publically challenging the traditions he now embraces.

SHE turns and heads off to her room, dragging him along with her. They are pre-teens. SHE sits him in her room and speaks to him.

SHE   I haven't said anything to Mom or Dad yet, but I have decided, that I will *not* be doing my Bat Mitzvah.

HE   Why?!

SHE   Because, it's a hypocrisy! Did you know that I can do a great job of my Bat Mitzvah but then I'm never allowed to read from the Torah ever again! Did you know that?! I'm not even allowed to touch a Torah! At Hebrew school we had this Rabbi came to speak and I went to shake his hand and he wouldn't even touch me! Because maybe possibly I might be having my period and be unclean?! Isn't that disgusting?! What is the point in doing a Bat Mitzvah if the only thing I'm going to be allowed to do is clean up after Pesach!? Can't you see how unfair that is?!

Beat.

HE   What's a period?

SHE stares at him. No answer.

Back to adults.

SHE   So I would like to ask all of you, to please now focus on my baby brother – for a change. (*SHE laughs.*) And as I raise this glass, on behalf of myself... and... my lover... Gloria.

HE turns in shock. SHE continues, very apprehensive, but determined.

She's sitting right over there – she was not invited to join us, at the head table – so please join me in a toast to my baby brother! L'Chaim!!

DANCE OF SIBS 4

SHE spins to face him. SHE's relieved, and a bit drunk. HE just looks at her, unmoving. SHE does the moves to the Dance of Sibs enthusiastically. HE just stands there not joining her.

Finally, HE sharply turns away. SHE stops.

They become adults in the first scene.

HE   OK look, um, I don't know how we're going to solve this. Um.

SHE   Well, it's not rocket science, we'll solve it.

HE   No it's not rocket science but it's got to get done.

SHE   Well, why don't you give me a list of things I have to do in the next few days. If it's phone calls I'm happy// to do phone calls–

HE   Do you know what has to be done?

SHE   No.

HE   Right. OK.

SHE   Well, that's why I'm asking you.

HE   OK but see part of what I'm asking you for, is that I don't want to have to do all of the thinking. Right? If we were here together, if the two of us could just sit down together, and together make a list, figure it out. I have no problem with doing half of it, that's not my problem, it's, my problem is me having to do all of the thinking, and then *delegating* it to you. Besides there's some stuff that is just here – like this house, and everything that's in it.

SHE   I don't want to do that right now.

HE   Well, when would you want to do it?

SHE   I don't – gee, I don't know.

           Pause.

           Transition.

           They greet each other at Pesach. They're now in their mid-thirties.

           They embrace as per their ritual, but much more reserved.

HE   Hey.

SHE   Hey.

HE   Happy Pesach.

SHE   To you too.

           They peck cheeks.

           Uncomfortable pause.

BOTH   How's work?

HE   (*simultaneous*) Great.

SHE   (*simultaneous*) Good.

BOTH   You?

SHE   (*simultaneous*) Fine.

HE   (*simultaneous*) Oĸ.

           Pause.

SHE   You're looking good, there, Mr. Vice-President.

HE   *Regional* Vice-President.

SHE   Yeah? Sorry. Whatever.

Pause.

HE   Oh you are so skinny.

SHE   Aw come on. (*beat*) It's all the travelling.

HE   Uh huh?

SHE   I got sick in Thailand.

HE   Oh no.

SHE   Yeah. (*beat*) Getting tired of the travelling.

HE   Oh yeah?

SHE   Mind you it does have its perks. I got to take Mom and Dad to New York for that gala thing...

HE   Oh yes, I heard all about it.

SHE   Oh. Great.

They sit.

SHE   Mom spent a fortune on clothes. She looks good though, don't you think?

HE   (*unsure*) Yeah.

SHE   Dad looks good, too.

HE   I think retirement suits him.

SHE   Cowboy boots?

They have a quick little laugh. Pause.

SHE   Listen, // I just got this letter–

HE   Look, Mom just sent me this letter––

SHE   –from Mom...

*HE pulls out a letter. SHE also does, and then
they exchange the letters, moving downstage, and
surreptitiously glancing behind them to make sure
they're not overheard. They read each other's letters.
Exchange furtive looks.*

Pause. They begin in a whisper.

HE   What are you going to do?

SHE   Don't look at me.

HE   I'm really worried about her.

SHE   What do you mean?

HE   She's getting old. I think she might be getting
Alzheimer's or something.

SHE   Stop that!

HE   She's forgetful, she tells you the same story over and
over–

SHE   She does that to you too?!

HE   Yeah.

SHE   That drives me crazy!

HE   And she calls me all the time at work.

SHE   All of a sudden she has so much to talk about – and
now this.

HE   You know, I hate the idea of her talking to a therapist
about me.

SHE   She has a lesbian daughter, in film. She's not talking
about *you*.

HE   So what are we going to do?

SHE   Well, we have to respond in some way.

HE	I don't want to have lunch with her and you and me and "talk about our feelings."
SHE	Maybe if we take her to lunch and tell her we don't want to talk about our feelings.
HE	Yeah. Because there's nothing to talk about.
SHE	Exactly.
HE	I mean, do you have any "unresolved issues?"
SHE	Not that I want to resolve. (*beat*) So what do we do?
HE	Well, we can just do nothing.
SHE	What?! We can't do that. She must know we got the letters by now. She'll be so embarrassed.
HE	Or... she'll forget.
SHE	You *want* her to have Alzheimer's!
HE	No. She'll forget. Or if she doesn't forget, maybe she'll be happy if we don't say anything, maybe she regrets writing the letters to us in the first place, maybe she doesn't really want to talk about it, it's just this therapy thing.
SHE	...I don't know.
HE	Look, how about we do nothing and if–
SHE	–she says something, then–
HE	–we'll say something.
HE	(*simultaneous*) Yeah!
SHE	(*simultaneous*) Good!
	SHE goes and sits down.
SHE	(*simultaneous*) Yes.

HE   (*simultaneous*) Good.

             Pause.

SHE   So, how's my niece?

             Transition.

             SHE becomes a baby.

SHE   Up up up up.

             HE lifts her up, slings her on his hip, and talks on a cell phone.

HE   Hello? Oh, hi.

SHE   (*as baby*) Hi. Hi.

HE   How are you? Oh yeah, she's getting big! Yeah, she looks just like you. Do you want to say hello to her? Say hello to your Aunt. (*HE holds the phone to the baby's mouth. SHE stops saying "hi" at that moment. HE takes the phone back.*) She was saying hi just a second ago.

SHE   (*as baby*) Hi.

HE   What? When? Tomorrow? No I can't. It's her birthday tomorrow, remember? Tomorrow at 3:30 I'm going to have 20 little girls running around this place. Why can't you do it?!

             SHE screams as the baby.

SHE   I – I – I – I–

             SHE grabs the phone and becomes an adult. HE turns his back to the audience and becomes an officious film crew person.

             I – I – I – I can't! Because I'm in Hungary. There's no physical way I could be there by tomorrow at 3:30. Yeah, but do you know what I had to do to get this appointment with the specialist? I just need you to go there with her and Dad, and ask for these three tests for her... because I don't want Dad to know what the tests are. Because he'll freak out. Yeah, I know, but we were supposed to have wrapped here yesterday and I am stuck – but that's why I need you to – but you – you – you – you–

HE takes the phone. SHE becomes the baby again.

SHE Ooo – ooo – ooo.

HE Look, I gotta go now, she's fussing.

SHE (*as baby*) Bye bye.

HE Ok. Ok! I'll do it. Well, I guess I'll just have to miss my own daughter's birthday party, won't I? Ok. Do you wanna say goodbye to her? Here. (*SHE stops saying "bye-bye" at that moment.*) She was saying bye a second ago.

SHE (*as soon as HE pulls the phone away*) Bye bye.

HE Ok bye. (*HE hangs up. SHE starts to scream.*) Who's Daddy's girl?

SHE AHHHH! (*SHE pulls at his hair or ear.*)

HE Who's Daddy's beautiful, clever, ow, precious girl?

SHE MOMMY!

HE Mommy's not here.

SHE MOMMY!

HE Shh Shh.

HE puts her down. They are adults in their late thirties.

Pause.

What a Happy Pesach.

SHE   I'm sorry. She just looks so...

HE   Yeah. Well, we have to do something.

SHE   Clearly. (*beat*) OK why don't I come home on the weekends, can you stay over sometimes during the week?

HE   Are you serious?

SHE   Or get a nurse part time?

HE   She needs to be in a home.

SHE   Not yet!

HE   She needs 24-hour-a-day care.

SHE   We can handle it!

HE   What do you mean "we," white man? I'm here, you're 400 miles away. I just got this promotion with more responsibility, Rochelle's past her due date, we have a three year old, we're renovating–

SHE   OK. Dad and I will handle it.

HE   Dad can't handle anything. (*beat*) She needs to be in a home.

> *SHE turns away, starting to cry. HE exits. SHE remains. HE stops.*
>
> *HE returns and stands in the doorway.*

Come on. Come on. We're gonna do the Afikoman now.

> *HE starts to go. SHE gets up.*

SHE   I'll move back home.

> *HE spins to look at her. Transition.*
>
> *They are pre-teens. HE points at her.*
>
> *This scene is punctuated with strong musical hits.*

HE   Hey! That's my shirt.

SHE   I know. Looks good on me doesn't it?

HE   It's mine! Take it off!

SHE   You were throwing it out. I found it in the Goodwill bag.

HE   I don't care. It's mine! You can't have it.

SHE   What is your problem? You've never even worn this shirt! You were getting rid of it. You were going to give it to a homeless person. Why can't I have it? You are such a jerk. What is your problem?!

> *Beat.*

HE   It's mine.

> *They look at each other, then HE addresses the Unseen Judge as SHE watches him for a moment.*
>
> *// indicates where they overlap.*

HE   When my mother... our mother died – after a person dies you sit Shiva, which lasts seven or eight days, I can't remember...

SHE   There are seven days of mourning. Shiva, from the Hebrew word Shevah, meaning seven. A group of men, traditionally, ten men, form a minyan, minyan "meaning" ten// and they say this prayer.

HE   It's like the Jewish version of a wake. It's a party really. The family all sits on these low stools, and you cover the mirrors// and you're encouraged to talk about the person who's died. It's really very beautiful.

SHE
So it was totally silent except for the sound of the men saying this prayer. Now traditionally, it is the men who say it. This *is* Judaism, the religion that gave us the prayer "thank god I was not born a woman" and the "you have to marry your rapist" laws, so anyway, well, // I happen to be the only one of the two of us who actually knows Hebrew and who excuse me, gives a shit, about prayer. So I joined in. Discreetly.

HE
She has a way, my sister, of making everything about her. And this is my mother... our mother, who died. A woman who didn't like to make waves; who knew there was a time // and a place for everything. And a funeral or a *wedding* is not exactly the time to make a strong feminist statement!

SHE
If God cares about what gender you are when you mourn I will be seriously disappointed. My mother rai–, our mother raised us to be equals, and was quite feminist in her own way, and she would have *wanted* me to say Kadish for her. And for my brother–

HE
I didn't say anything–

SHE
–out of everyone–

HE
–I didn't want to make a scene–

SHE
–to be the one to give me dirty looks–

HE
–I'm not going to change her now–

SHE
–at the funeral for my mother–

HE
–we're both too old to change.

SHE
–like he was the head of the family.

Pause.

They look at each other, then look out to the Unseen Judge again and speak the last speeches simultaneously.

SHE   I mean, he doesn't even know the words, but he started to pray louder, like he wanted to be the big man, so he chose this funeral to try and become the older sibling. So I prayed louder to drown out the mumbo jumbo pathetic attempt at Hebrew, which was totally inappropriate, especially in front of Uncle Joey and all the men!

HE   There are some traditions in Judaism that have survived for thousands of years for a reason, and yes it's a patriarchal religion, but it doesn't matter how hard she tries, she will never be a man. I mean, she was almost shouting to drown us out. It was ridiculous, and embarrassing and totally inappropriate especially in front of the whole family!

        Beat.

SHE   What he did...

HE   I don't think she knows how // unfair it was.

SHE   ...was not fair.

        Transition.

        They are slightly older.

        They speak on the phone. It is Pesach again.

HE   Hey.

SHE   Hey.

HE   Happy Pesach.

SHE   To you too.

HE   How *are* you?

SHE   Good! (*Pause.*) Dad sounds great. He seems really happy.

HE   Did you talk to Cherise?

SHE	Yes. She's hilarious. I love the way she bosses him around, it's hysterical.
HE	Yeah. Well, she's not like mom was, that's for sure.
	Pause.
SHE	So, it sounds like Rochelle's new business is doing very well.
HE	Oh yeah. She's working 20-hour days seven days a week. We never see each other.
SHE	Good for her. (*Pause.*) So, are you still not smoking?
HE	No, I started again.
SHE	Aw, well.
HE	You?
SHE	Aw, I don't really miss it.
HE	Good for you. (*Pause.*) Did Dad tell you he's going to Florida again this year, this time with Cherise?
SHE	Yeah. Suzanna and I are going down for a week.
HE	You are?
SHE	Yeah. You know, you should go. You should bring the girls. It's very nice.
HE	Well, between my work and Rochelle's work and the girls' extra-curricular activities–
SHE	Do you need money?
HE	No. Thank you.
	Pause.
SHE	(*simultaneously*) So how's the–

HE   (*simultaneously*) So what are you–

Oh sorry. Go ahead.

SHE   You go.

HE   No, go.

SHE   You go.

HE   Go.

SHE   Go go.

HE   (*in reference to the plasticine scene*) Go go go go go go.

> *Beat. HE smiles at the memory. SHE is still and saddened. HE waits for her to laugh with him. SHE doesn't.*

So, how's the new house?

SHE   We're renovating...

> *Pause.*

> *They each wait for the other to pick up the ball.*

So, Dad tells me he let you lead the Seder this year.

HE   Yeah finally.

SHE   Ha.

HE   I tried to move it along a little bit.

SHE   Ha. Ha.

HE   Oh, and you should have heard the Four Questions. The girls did them together.// They were so cute.

SHE   They did them together?! Oh! That must take the pressure off.

HE   Yeah. (*beat*) So, do you think you might be able to make it in next year? You haven't been in for Pesach in a long time. Do you think it's possible you could rearrange// your schedule–

SHE   Hey. Have you done the Afikoman yet?

HE   No, we're just about to do it.

SHE   Oh, well, you know where you have to hide it, right?

HE   Yes.

　　　　They speak simultaneously.

SHE   Behind the thing, under the cushions.

HE   Behind the couch, under the pillows.

　　　　Pause.

　　　　So how's// Suzann–

SHE   OK bye.

　　　　Beat. A suspended moment.

HE   Well, goodbye then.

　　　　Beat.

SHE   I gotta get back to the drywall.

HE   Yeah. Well, thanks for uh// calling.

SHE   OK.

HE   Take care of// yours–

SHE   Bye.

　　　　Transition.

> *They are in their forties. They return to the first scene*
> *of the play. They stand in the doorway together for a*
> *moment. HE looks at her, but SHE is looking away.*
> *HE continues to look at her. SHE sighs. HE walks into*
> *the living room and sits.*
>
> *Pause.*

HE   OK look, um, I don't know how we're going to solve
this. Um.

SHE   Well, it's not rocket science, we'll solve it.

HE   No it's not rocket science but it's got to get done.

SHE   Well, why don't you give me a list of things I have
to do in the next few days. If it's phone calls I'm
happy / / to do phone calls–

HE   Do you know what has to be done?

SHE   No.

HE   Right. OK.

SHE   Well, that's why I'm asking you.

HE   OK but see part of what I'm asking you for, is that
I don't want to have to do all of the thinking. Right?

> *SHE comes into the room and stands by her chair.*

If we were here together, if the two of us could just sit
down together, and together make a list, figure it out.
I have no problem with doing half of it, that's not my
problem, it's, my problem is me having to do all of
the thinking, and then *delegating* it to you. Besides
there's some stuff that is just here – like this house,
and everything that's in it.

> *Beat. SHE looks at him, shocked.*

SHE   I don't want to do *that* right now.

HE   Then when would you want to do it?

SHE   I don't – gee I don't know.

HE   (*laughs*) Well then it's a little hard to kind of–

SHE   What is your rush?

HE   Because it's got to get done. As I said before, there are certain things that are time sensitive. We have to get the death certif–

SHE   And there are certain things that are not time sensitive.

HE   That's true, but there are certain things that are. Like I'm sure Cherise is not going to be clamouring down our neck for the twenty-five thousand dollars that Dad left for her in his will, but at some point we're going to have to give it to her, it's Dad's last// wish.

SHE   We'll give it to her then! That's fine.

HE   Yeah but in order for her to get the money – there are–

SHE   Look, I don't want–

HE   –certain things that have to be done like we have to *sell* this house.

          Pause. SHE looks at him.

          Fine. Go. I'll do it.

SHE   No, I'm not asking you to do it on your own, I'm just saying I need a couple of weeks. I don't want to go through their *stuff* right now.

          SHE sits.

HE   Oᴋ fine. So meanwhile there's the death certificate, and the will being probated, and opening up a bank account for the estate, and it goes on and on and on and it all has to happen in a certain order or it just falls apart, right? It all has to happen in a certain way.

SHE   You know, people have done this before us.

HE   Yes absolutely, but usually the co-executors are *legally* responsible / / to do it.

SHE   (*in a laugh*) Pfff.

HE   Ok look, I'm not going to have a fight with you. That's not what I want to do.

SHE   I think that is what you want to do.

HE   Our father just died and I don't want to–

SHE   You know what? I think that *is* what you want to do.

HE   What? Why are you–

SHE   Because you're acting like you want to have a fight with me!

HE   I'm not. Excuse me, I'm just a little shocked / / that you would just take off the day after–

SHE   Well I'm just a little shocked that you would–

HE   –Shiva when there's all this stuff left to do and you're just assuming that *I* will do it.

SHE   No I'm not! You're not listening to me! I don't want you to do it. I'm just saying I need a couple of weeks. Just give me a couple of weeks. I can't – I can't do this right now!

                SHE starts to go.

HE   But some of it can't wait a couple of weeks, that's what I've been trying to say. Some of it can't wait. Some of it *has to be done now. Now.*

SHE   I don't think you're right.

HE   Well, do you want to call the lawyer and ask?

SHE   Sure!

HE   I've been speaking to him. This is what he said to me, he said, you know, take it easy, but it's got to get done. We have to go in – well, do you want me to make you a list, I'll make you a list.

SHE   Make me a list!

HE   Fine.

> *HE does. SHE watches him in disbelief.*
>
> *Pause.*

SHE   Well, this is just pretty shocking.

HE   What's "shocking?"

SHE   That that's what you care about right now.

HE   It's not what I care about.

SHE   Well, it's your priority.

HE   Excuse me, that's why I didn't do it during Shiva. This is why–

SHE   You were just waiting for he second that Shiva was over to just pounce!

HE   Nooo! I assumed you were staying for several more days. I didn't want to do it during Shiva, I wanted to do it–

SHE   Just the day after Shiva!

HE   Well, to get started on it, not to – you're misinterpreting what I'm saying.

> *Beat.*

HE   What do you think I am?

                Beat.

SHE   Well...

                Beat.

HE   (*a real question*) What do you think I am?

SHE   I think... you're being very insensitive. I don't actually know what I think you are right now, actually! I am not going through their *stuff* like a couple of *vultures* saying I want this I want that, you have that I'll take this, let's sell this and make a few bucks! I'm not doing that!

HE   You think that's what I'm saying? Is that what you truly think that's what I'm saying?

SHE   Well that what it sounds like!

HE   It's just *stuff* that needs doing, it's part of the every day / / stuff of life–

SHE   And I am *telling you* I can't do this right now!

HE   Fine. / / Then *you* go home–

SHE   I need to go home!

HE   –and I WILL DO IT!!!

                Beat.

SHE   You've got your family and your kids–

HE   Right.

SHE   –and you've got everything here, and do you know I've been here alone? Do you know that? I've been here alone this whole time. You always had your kids to go home to and your family to go home to and all these people here to talk to who know you.

HE   Yeah, right.

SHE   They don't know me here. My whole life is in another
           city. You know, my whole *life* is in another city! I can't
           stay here any more. I've been completely alone!
           Thank you!

           Long pause.

HE   I think Rochelle and I are splitting up.

           Beat.

           I think that's what's going on here. I **don't** have
           anybody to go home and talk to. And I'm sorry that
           you're not at home and you don't have all of your
           "support systems" and that kind of stuff, but I'm
           under stress as well.

           SHE nods but says nothing.

           I just thought that we could spend some time
           together.

           SHE gives him a sharp look.

           This is a chance – I mean, I don't know, you've been
           away, you've had your own life, you haven't kind of
           cared about what goes on in my life–

SHE   That's not true!

HE   Come on. Come on. Be honest. You haven't come in
           for Pesach in I don't know how long. How often do
           we speak?

SHE   Well, how often do you call me?!

HE   Well, I tried calling you but it always felt like I was
           bugging you, / / so I backed off.

SHE   Do you know that when you call me you don't ask
           me a thing about my life?

HE   What?!

SHE   Do you know that? You've yet to ask me one thing
          about my life!// You don't ask me you don't–

HE   I ask you about work all the time//

SHE   –you don't ask me about work. You don't *ask* me. You
          don't *really* ask me. You don't ask me about my life.
          You don't want to *know* about... my girlfriend.

HE   Wha–?!

SHE   I *always* ask you about Rochelle, and about your kids,
          and about what's going on with you and you never
          ask me! What is the point in talking on the phone
          with you – it's like two idiot strangers talking on the
          phone. Really. I mean admit it. You know what, admit
          it. Why can't you admit it? Why can't you admit
          what our phone calls are like?! Why can't you admit
          that we don't have anything to say to each other?!
          That's what you want?!

HE   No.

SHE   That's what you *really* want?!

HE   No!

SHE   You want me to sit around here with you for another
          week? *Another* week! Like this past week?! (*beat*) "You
          know, Rochelle and I are splitting up." I'm very sorry
          for you, but–

HE   (*laughs*) Gee thanks. You've always hated her guts
          anyways.

SHE   You know what, I like Rochelle, actually.

HE   *Now* you like her.

SHE   I do!

HE   Probably because she's splitting up with me.

SHE   I'm not thinking that deeply about it.

          Pause.

HE   You know every time I try and ask about you, try
          to get at your stuff, you always, always... don't go
          there. You don't want to go. I try and open up the
          conversation and it's like you don't want to tell me
          what's going on, so I gave up after a while.

SHE   Try me!

HE   OK. What's going on with your life? Are you and
          Suzanna still together, I don't even know that!
          I heard you were having a bit of a problem, are
          you together or not, what?!

SHE   Oh boy, that's really nice, it really makes me want to
          talk about it.

HE   There you go.

SHE   "Are you together or what?"

          HE laughs.

          "I heard you were breaking up, are you together or
          not, what?" And that implies that I just – I mean you
          are punishing me with everything you say!

HE   But I try and tell *you*!! You never volunteer *anything*!
          You never say "this is what's going on with me."

SHE   (*simply*) We're not friends.

          Pause.

          They are both taken aback by what SHE's said.

HE   Clearly.

          Pause.

SHE   (*sincerely*) And it's half my fault, I know.... We're not....
And I don't know what to do about it.

   Pause.

HE   Can't we be friends?

SHE   ...I don't know.

   Pause.

   They're on the verge of dissolving.

HE   They're dead.

   Pause.

   They're dead. It's just you and me.

   Pause. They look at each other.

   SHE reaches out to him.

SHE   Dance.

   *SHE is a toddler and he's a baby. SHE takes his hand
   and speaks to the audience, gently.*

SHE   This is my new baby sister, Cindy... dance.

   They dance, SHE circling him. As they turn, they age.

   *They become seniors, in their eighties. They greet each
   other, gingerly kissing cheeks, and begin to slowly
   dance.*

   HE pulls away and looks at her.

HE   I want you to make me a promise.

SHE   Mhm?

HE   If I'm lying there, all full of tubes, I want you to
promise me... you'll kill me.

SHE   (*beat*) Oĸ.

HE   You'll kill me?

SHE   I'll shoot you.

HE   No! I don't want anything violent.

SHE   I'll push you out a window.

HE   No, I want it to be peaceful.

SHE   I'll hire someone!

HE   No! I don't want a stranger! I want you to do it.

SHE   I'll hire someone, he'll come with a wire, put it around your neck, pull, slice, like a piece of cheese.

HE   I want to be asleep.

SHE   You won't even know it's coming.

HE   You promise?

SHE   Yeah.

> *They resume dancing. Then SHE pulls away and looks at him.*

SHE   I don't want you killing me.

HE   Oĸ.

SHE   (*fondly*) Because you'll screw it up.

> *Beat.*

BOTH   Yeah.

> *They continue dancing as the lights fade.*
>
> *The end.*

Diane Flacks and Richard Greenblatt wear many hats in theatre, television, film and radio. They are not siblings.